MONGOLIA

MONGOLIA

Rebecca Stefoff

CHELSEA HOUSE

LV2-005086

Library of Congress Cataloging-in-Publication Data

Stefoff, Rebecca.
  Mongolia.
  Includes index.
  Summary: An introduction to the history, topography, economy,
politics, industry, people, and culture of the rugged country lying
between Russia and China.

  1. Mongolia.   [1. Mongolia]
  I. Title.   II. Series.
  DS798.S74   1986   951'.73   86-11686

  ISBN 1-55546-153-0

Editorial Director: Susan R. Williams
Associate Editor: Rafaela Ellis
Art Director: Maureen McCafferty
Series Designer: Anita Noble
Project Coordinator: Kathleen P. Luczak

ACKNOWLEDGEMENTS

The author and publishers are grateful to these organizations for information and photographs: Mongolian Mission to the United Nations; *National Geographic* Magazine, for six
photographs by Dean Conger © National Geographic Society; National Zoological Park,
Washington, D.C.; Photo Researchers, Inc., for photographs by George Holton and Char-
bonnier; Smithsonian Institution; United Nations; Woodland Park Zoological Gardens,
Seattle, for a photograph by Joseph L. Fox; World Health Organization. Picture research:
Imagefinders, Inc.

Contents

Map 6

Between Old and New 9

The Great Khans 18

The Mongolian Revolution 28

Land of the Blue Sky 35

The Gobi Desert 41

The People of Mongolia 48

Government and Education 57

Ulan Bator and Other Cities 65

Resources, Economy, and Communication 70

Culture and Customs 79

Ways of Life Today 87

Index 93

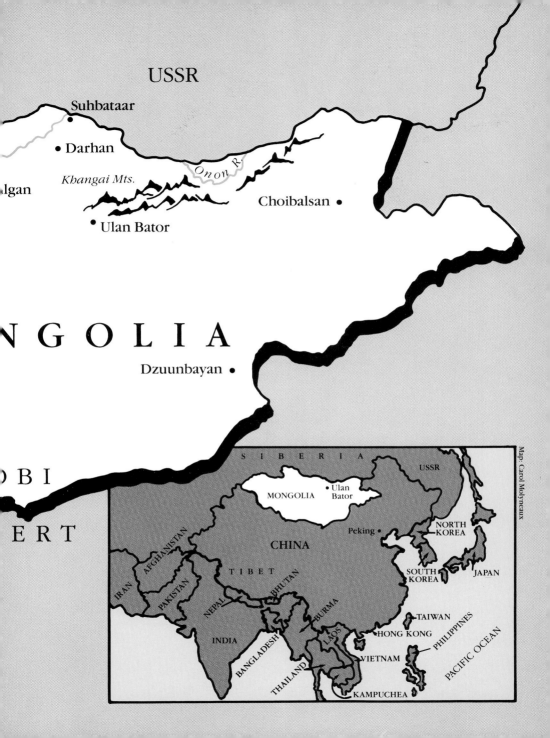

USSR

• Suhbataar

• Darhan

Khangai Mts.

Onon R.

lgan

Choibalsan •

• Ulan Bator

NGOLIA

Dzuunbayan •

OBI

ERT

S I B E R I A

MONGOLIA

• Ulan Bator

USSR

CHINA

Peking •

NORTH KOREA

AFGHANISTAN

TIBET

BHUTAN

SOUTH KOREA

JAPAN

IRAN

PAKISTAN

NEPAL

BURMA

HONG KONG

TAIWAN

PHILIPPINES

INDIA

BANGLADESH

LAOS

VIETNAM

PACIFIC OCEAN

THAILAND

KAMPUCHEA

Map: Carol Molyneaux

Ornate Chinese clothing was the fashion for upper-class Mongolian women in the late 19th century

Between Old and New

Mongolia is an ancient land lying in the heart of northern central Asia, between Russia and China. It is sparsely populated and rugged, with mountains in the north, grassy plains (known as steppes) in the central regions, and the Gobi Desert in the south. Its people combine the racial and cultural characteristics of the Chinese, the Siberians, and the Russian and Turkish peoples of central Asia. They speak the Mongol language, which has changed little over the centuries.

Three or four thousand years ago, the area now known as Mongolia was the homeland of many tribes who spread out in all directions and populated vast areas of Asia, including parts of Turkey, Russia, Persia (now called Iran), Afghanistan, and China. The tribespeople who remained in the ancestral homeland were wandering herdsmen and warriors, famed for their skilled horsemanship and archery. They came to be known as the Mongols. Over time, as they dominated and absorbed neighboring tribes, their territory grew and was called Mongolia.

Mongolia has had a long and turbulent history. At one time, the Mongol clans were united under the great warlord Genghis Khan. He and his successors ruled the Mongol Empire, which

stretched from Peking in the east to the plains of Hungary on the edge of Europe, and from Siberia in the north to the regions that are now Iran, Afghanistan, and Pakistan in the south. It was the largest land empire in all of history.

After the death of Genghis Khan and his sons, however, the empire began to break up. Eventually Mongolia was conquered by

Old meets new in Hatgal, where traditional ger dwellings are equipped with electricity and televisions

Elderly women sit and chat in a village square

the Chinese and divided into two regions. One of these regions, known as Inner Mongolia, lay to the south of the Gobi Desert and is now part of China. The larger region, which was called Outer Mongolia, contains most of the original Mongol homeland. This region is now an independent nation called the Mongolian People's Republic. Today, the name "Mongolia" refers only to the Mongolian People's Republic.

Mongolia is the shape of a long oval, about 1,500 miles from east to west and 780 miles from north to south at the widest point. It covers 604,000 square miles (1,565,000 square kilometers), roughly the size of North and South Dakota, Wyoming, Colorado, Montana, Kansas and Nebraska combined. The population is just under two million, or slightly less than three people per square mile. Although the population is increasing rapidly, Mongolia still has fewer people per square mile than most countries in the world and fewer than any other Asian country.

During much of modern history, Mongolia was a mysterious place, sealed off from the rest of the world by the forbidding wastelands of central Asia—cliffs, arid plateaus, deserts, and vast uninhabited tracts. The famous Italian trader and explorer Marco Polo reached Mongolia and met Genghis Khan's descendant, Kublai Khan, but few other Westerners visited the remote, bar-

Although collective farms have changed the herding industry, many herdsmen still dress as their ancestors did

baric home of the Mongols. When the Chinese controlled all of Mongolia in the 18th and 19th centuries, they closed it to the outside world. As a result, little was known of modern Mongolia until the Mongolian People's Republic achieved independence with the help of the Soviet Union in 1921.

Marco Polo's arrival at Kublai Khan's court in Peking is illustrated in an old etching

Mongolia now has a communist system of government. It has many treaties and other close ties with the Soviet Union. The northern border with the Soviet Union makes up almost 40 percent of Mongolia's total boundary. The remaining 60 percent is the border shared with the People's Republic of China. In disputes

between its two giant neighbors, Mongolia today sides with the Soviet Union. Russian troops assist the Mongolian army in patrolling the Chinese-Mongolian frontier.

Since 1921, the main goal of the Mongolian government has been to bring the country into the 20th century. This has not been an easy task.

At the time of the Mongolian Revolution in 1921, the population of the country numbered only 650,000. Less than 2 percent of the people could read and write. The economy was based on a centuries-old system of livestock breeding and barter. There were very few city dwellers. Almost all Mongolians were nomads who lived in traditional round tents called *gers* (*yurts* in Russian) and moved with the seasons across the pasturelands of the steppes. There was no industry and no schooling. Health care did not exist, and disease threatened the Mongolian people with extinction. Despite a proud history and a rich folk culture, Mongolia was a primitive, backward land.

Today, Mongolia is being transformed by the government, which is guided by the Mongolian People's Revolutionary Party, or MPRP. Along with the increase in population, cities have grown greatly. New towns and cities are being built throughout Mongolia. Nearly half of the country's population now lives in urban centers. Industry has been introduced, usually with the help of the Soviet Union, and state-sponsored health care is available to all Mongolians. Almost everyone in Mongolia can now read and write.

The rapid pace of change in Mongolia has created a country with a split personality. Many ancient customs and ways of life persist strongly, giving Mongolia an inescapable flavor of the past. For example, it is not unusual to see sturdy Mongol horses, whose shaggy ancestors carried Genghis Khan into battle, tethered outside high-rise apartment buildings in the capital city of Ulan Bator.

At the same time, Mongolia's modernization program has made it one of the fastest-growing and most economically stable countries in Asia or in the communist bloc. Increasing prosperity has changed many aspects of daily life for the Mongolian people. One example of these changes is in housing. The traditional ger remains the most popular form of dwelling, but many gers now have electricity and radios. The MPRP hopes to continue developing the country and improving the standard of living for its people, while preserving Mongolia's unique traditions and heritage.

To understand how the old and the new are intermingled in present-day Mongolia, we must first look more closely at its history.

The Great Khans

The earliest historical mention of the Mongol people occurs in a Chinese chronicle dating from approximately 1500 B.C. The Mongols were one of many groups of northern barbarians who periodically attacked China. The Great Wall of China was built to keep them from invading the settled lands to the south. In the 4th century B.C., a tribe called the Hsiung-nu, or Huns, formed a loose confederation of tribes in what is now Mongolia. After several centuries of civil war and fighting with the neighboring Chinese, the Hsiung-nu confederation broke up. Some of the tribes settled in China. Others migrated far west, to appear in Europe in the 5th century A.D. as the Huns of Attila.

In Mongolia itself, one tribe after another achieved power, only to give way to new alliances among the warring clans. The Mongol way of life continued from generation to generation with little change. The people roamed the grassy steppes as nomadic herdsmen, with large flocks of sheep and goats and herds of cattle and yaks (large, hairy oxen which live at high altitudes throughout much of central Asia). In the southern part of Mongolia, herds of two-humped camels were kept. Camel caravans traveled well-worn routes from oasis to oasis across the desert.

18

Since the days of the great khans, camels have been an important part of life for nomads in the Gobi Desert; they transport goods for long distances, although Mongolians do not ride them

19

Even more important to the Mongols than their sheep and cattle were their horses. The Mongolian horse is tireless, strong and wiry, about the size of an American pony. A Mongol's wealth was measured by the number of horses he owned. Horses also contributed an important food item—*airak,* a mildly alcoholic beverage made from fermented mare's milk, which remains the staple drink of Mongolia today.

The Mongols were magnificent horsemen. It was sometimes said of them that they were born in the saddle. Even young boys

Mongolians can take their gers with them when they move to new locations

could ride and could shoot the large, heavy Mongol bow with great accuracy from horseback.

The Mongol Way of Life

The nomadic way of life did not simply mean aimless wandering. Instead, groups of nomads traveled from one established campground to another, usually returning to their starting point within a few years. Each family lived in a large ger that had collapsible supports like the ribs of an umbrella. Its walls were made of felt, a material invented in Mongolia. When the tribes moved to fresh grazing grounds, they carried the gers in large carts pulled by yaks or oxen. There was little agriculture. The Mongol diet consisted mostly of meat and dairy products; indeed, a Mongol proverb says, "Grass for beasts, meat for men."

The early Mongol religion was a form of shamanism. This means that mountains, animals, and other natural objects were believed to be inhabited by spirits. Tengri, the sky-god, was the chief deity. Shamans, or medicine men, could supposedly contact Tengri and other spirits. Often the shamans had much political power.

The elaborate social structure of the Mongols was based on blood relationships, or clans, which joined together to form tribes. Each tribe contained aristocratic princes, common people, and slaves. The slaves were usually captured members of other tribes. From time to time, the princes of several clans or tribes would elect a *khan,* or warlord. The khans fought among themselves for supremacy. This was the situation in Mongolia when its greatest leader, Temujin, came to power early in the 13th century A.D.

Born in 1162, Temujin was the great-grandson of a strong khan. He inherited many blood-feuds and quickly proved himself a master warrior and politician. He used raids, marriage alliances, and tribal treaties to raise his own tribe to a position of leadership. In 1206, at a *kuriltai* or tribal assembly, the khans of all the Mongol tribes proclaimed Temujin to be Genghis (or Chingiz) Khan, which means "universal monarch."

Not content with rulership of the Mongols, Genghis set out to expand his territory. First he consolidated Mongol control over the forest-dwelling tribes of Siberia and the nomads of the western steppes. Then he turned his attention to China. His troops broke through the Great Wall and overran the plains of northern China, capturing Peking. Genghis then led his horsemen far to the southwest, capturing and pillaging lands all the way to Persia and the Caspian Sea. By the time of his death in 1227, he had forged the Mongol tribes into the greatest conquering army the world had ever seen.

Genghis's military might did not lie in large numbers. His army probably contained only 200,000 men at its largest. However, they were organized, disciplined, and fearless. Soldiers wore a type of armor called *lamellar,* invented in the Orient. It was made of leather strips covered with lacquer to keep out water. Each soldier carried an enormous bow, as well as a lance or curved sword for close fighting. But the Mongol soldier's greatest advantage was his mobility. Each man in the army owned

These men display clothing and weaponry similar to that of Genghis Khan's day

between three and twenty horses, and he never rode the same horse for two days in a row. With fresh mounts and their heredi-tary skill on horseback, the Mongol brigades easily out-maneuvered larger but clumsier forces.

Under Genghis, the Mongols also became master strategists. They carried collapsible bridges, similar in construction to their gers, so that they could cross rivers at unexpected places. They often besieged cities for long periods, once diverting a river and creeping into a fortified city along the dry riverbed. In both strength and cunning they were invincible.

23

A noose on a pole is used to lasso horses

    With such a vast area to govern, Genghis faced the problem of communication over long distances. He solved it with a mail service called the "horse-post system." Along major caravan routes and other strategic roadways, local chieftains were ordered to maintain horses for the use of the Great Khan's special messengers. A good rider with a constant supply of fresh mounts could cover as much as 250 miles in one day. Genghis Khan's horse-post system was so efficient that it remained in use in Mongolia until 1949, when it was replaced by the telegraph and telephone.

    Much of what we know about the rise of the Mongol Empire comes from a remarkable book called *The Secret History of the Mongols.* Its author is unknown, but it is the oldest known document in the Mongol language. It was written sometime during the mid-1200s and gives many details of the Mongol way of life and of

Genghis Khan's career. It even recounts how, as a boy, Genghis tracked down and punished the horse-thieves who had made off with his family's herd of eight bay geldings.

On Genghis's death, the Mongol Empire was divided into four kingdoms or *khanates,* each ruled by one of his sons. The oldest son, Jochi, received western Siberia and southern Russia. Under his successors, the warlike Mongols and Russians of this region became known as the Golden Horde. The second son, Chagatai (or Jagatai), received central Asia between the Caspian Sea and the Tibetan plateau. The third son, Ogadai, received the western part of Mongolia. The youngest son, Tolui, received eastern Mongolia. Tolui's descendants also acquired Persia.

Of Genghis's four sons, Ogadai was named Great Khan. He continued to carry out his father's plans for the conquest of Russia and China. He also established a permanent capital at Karakorum, a site in north central Mongolia where tribal assemblies traditionally met and armies were mustered. Although the Mongols continued to live in gers, Karakorum contained many stone buildings and monuments and became a bustling market town and caravan center.

Ogadai ruled until 1241 and was succeeded by his son Guyuk, who died in 1248. The next Great Khan chosen was Mongke, a descendant not of Ogadai but of Tolui. Then, in 1260, Mongke's brother Kublai rose to power as Great Khan. The most famous Mongol leader after Genghis Khan, Kublai Khan extended the empire from Moscow to Canton and from Baghdad to Korea. Mongol dominion was at its greatest under Kublai Khan.

An ancient stone tortoise at Karakorum is the only surviving monument to Ogadai Khan's reign

Many innovations took place during Kublai's reign. He moved the capital of the Mongol World Empire from Karakorum to Peking, and he had many Chinese counselors. He also entertained several Europeans, including the Polos, at his magnificent court. It was at this time that the Tibetan form of Buddhism became the official religion of the Mongol aristocrats, although Buddhism had been known to the Mongols since the 8th or 9th century.

Kublai ruled both as Great Khan of the Mongol World Empire and as emperor of a new dynasty he founded in China. Not all of his ventures were successful, however. The Mongols tried to invade the island of Java, but were forced to withdraw after a skillful guerilla campaign by the Javanese ruler, Prince Wijaya. And in 1284, Kublai sent an immense Chinese armada to conquer Japan. A typhoon, celebrated in Japanese legend as the *kamikaze,* or

"divine wind," destroyed the fleet, and the Japanese captured all of the surviving Chinese and Mongol soldiers.

Kublai was the last of the Great Khans. After his death in 1294, his successors were unable to hold his huge empire together. The khans of the central and western portions of the empire fought among themselves while their khanates gradually developed into separate countries. The native Chinese had always resented their Mongol conquerors. Kublai's death sparked a series of uprisings throughout China, and by 1367 the Mongols had lost their foothold there. In 1382, a vengeful Chinese army destroyed the Mongol capital of Karakorum, and the very location of the city was forgotten for many years. Mongolia, no longer a great empire, ceased to play a major part in world history and faded into obscurity.

The Mongolian Revolution

Although the unity of the Mongol World Empire had been shattered by the end of the 13th century, the Chinese could not immediately gain complete control of the Mongol homelands. New tribes rose to power, many of them headed by chieftains who did not claim descent from Genghis. Several of these powerful khans tried to form a new Mongol empire or confederacy, but failed.

During the 14th century, one Mongol khan, Altan, reinforced Buddhism as the main Mongolian religion. He invited a high-ranking priest, or lama, from Tibet to lead the Buddhists in Mongolia. The lama's headquarters were in Urga, a small city in central Mongolia. He was given the title Dalai Lama, or "supreme lama." Although the spiritual leader of the Buddhists of Tibet is still called by this title, it was originally Mongolian. The successors of that first Dalai Lama in Mongolia were called "the Living Buddhas of Urga." Urga gradually became the capital of Mongolia.

The various Mongol tribes continued to wage war with China. By 1759, however, Mongolia was completely controlled by the rulers of China, the Manchu dynasty. Under the Manchus, the Buddhist lamas in Mongolia became very powerful. There were 750 monasteries scattered throughout Mongolia, and great numbers of the country's young men became Buddhist priests. Because the priests were not permitted to marry or father children, the population did not grow for several centuries. The lamas owned great herds of cattle and flocks of sheep, which were tended for them by servant herdsmen.

A small group of aristocrats (most of them Chinese) also owned much of the land in Mongolia. The native Mongolians were a subject people in their own homeland, and for several centuries they had almost no communication with the outside world.

During the 19th century, as the Russian empire expanded into Siberia under the rule of the tsars, Russia began to challenge China's ownership of Mongolia. Outer Mongolia, which was separated from China by the great natural barrier of the Gobi Desert, began to look toward Russia in the hope of assistance against the Manchus. A small group of Mongols even fled westward into Russia and settled along the Volga River. Their descendants, who still speak Mongolian and follow their ancient customs, live there today in what is called the Kalmuck Republic of the U.S.S.R.

Monks keep the ancient Buddhist tradition alive

A Mongolian woman wears a traditional sheep-horn headdress; the style of her costume means that she is married

Imperial Russia proved to be more interested in acquiring Mongolia for itself than in liberating it from China. The two giant countries schemed and fought for possession of the smaller land, but China was able to keep it for many years.

When revolution broke out in China in 1911, the people of Mongolia declared themselves independent, with the Living Buddha of Urga, the head of the Mongolian Buddhist church, as their leader. Most countries, however, continued to regard Mongolia as a province of China. Under the rule of the Living Buddha, little changed in Mongolian life. Lamas and nobles still held all of the

A portrait of Suhke Bator, one of the leaders of the Mongolian Revolution

country's wealth and power. Education was a closely guarded secret of the ruling elite. Many of the common people were discontented. When communist forces toppled the Russian tsar in the October Revolution of 1917, some Mongolian communists believed that a revolution should take place in Mongolia, too.

Heroes of the Revolution

Two men became revolutionary leaders among the Mongolians. Their names were Sukhe Bator and Choibalsan. Sukhe Bator had been a gunner in the Mongolian army until the Chinese disbanded

31

it. Choibalsan had been a Buddhist lama. Both of them led underground movements of political resistance against the Chinese, the Chinese-influenced Mongolian ruling class, and the remnants of pro-tsarist Russian nobility that had fled into Mongolia and persecuted the Mongolian people. Sukhe Bator and Choibalsan hoped to establish a modern, communist government that would reform land ownership and bring progress to the common people.

Horsemen on a plain near Ulan Bator, the capital city

The Mongolian Revolution was not very successful until Sukhe Bator sought aid from the Soviet Union. He rode north out of Mongolia with a secret message concealed in the handle of his riding whip. The message was a plea to Lenin, leader of the Soviets, asking for support. The plea was answered and on July 11, 1921, a joint force of Russian and Mongolian soldiers captured Urga. July 11 is celebrated every year as Mongolia's independence day. Urga remained the capital but was renamed Ulan Bator, which means "red hero." Inner Mongolia remained a part of China.

Sukhe Bator died in 1923. He is now regarded as Mongolia's greatest national hero, and there are many statues of him throughout the country. The Living Buddha died in 1924, and the Mongolian People's Republic was officially founded in October of that year. Choibalsan served as prime minister after 1939 and closed most Buddhist temples and monasteries.

After the revolution, many Mongol people who had been living in Inner Mongolia came to the Mongolian People's Republic. And large numbers of Chinese people who had been residents of Mongolia moved in the other direction, back across the frontier to China.

Mongolia became a member of the United Nations in 1961 and has diplomatic relationships with 52 countries. Although most of its treaties and trade relationships are with other communist countries, Mongolia is also developing some links with capitalist countries, including the United States. No longer a land of mystery, Mongolia is slowly becoming better known to the rest of the world.

A herd of Bactrian camels nibbles weeds in the semi-desert region

Land of the Blue Sky

In its terrain and climate, Mongolia is a little like Montana and the Dakotas in the United States. An especially outstanding feature is the number of clear, sunny days that the country enjoys each year—usually about 250 days without clouds or rainfall. Mongolia is sometimes called "The Land of the Blue Sky." Centuries ago, Genghis Khan described it as "the place of everlasting blue skies," according to *The Secret History of the Mongols*.

Of course, rain does fall in Mongolia, usually in the summer months. In fact, summer weather can be unpredictable, and sudden downpours sometimes cause severe floods. The annual rainfall ranges from 16 to 20 inches in the northern part of the country to 2 to 5 inches in the extreme south.

Winters are cold and summers are warm and mild in Mongolia. January temperatures can fall as low as –29 degrees Fahrenheit (–34 Centigrade) in the north and –2 (–19) in the south. In July, temperatures rise to 60 degrees Fahrenheit (15 degrees C) in the north and 75 (23) in the south. An unusual feature of the Mongolian climate is that temperatures can rise or fall as much as 55 degrees Fahrenheit (30 degrees C) in one day. These sudden and extreme variations in temperature create strong winds, and sandstorms or hailstorms may spring up without warning. Earthquakes are also common. Some of them are quite severe, although the low population density prevents them from doing great damage.

Mongolia's topography is varied, giving the country many different types of scenery (topography is a general term for all of the physical features of a place or region). The average altitude is 5,200 feet—nearly one mile—above sea level. In the mountain ranges of the northwest, however, many peaks tower to great heights. Some of them are covered with snow and ice year-round. The central and eastern parts of Mongolia are the steppes—vast, rolling plains. The southern third of the country consists of the Gobi plateau. Let's look more closely at each of these regions.

Three major mountain ranges thrust into Mongolia like long, narrow fingers from the north and west. For the most part, they are thickly forested, except at the highest points. The tallest and longest range, the Altai Mountains, is the farthest west. The main body of the range, the Mongol Altai, contains the highest peak in Mongolia. Its name is Monh Hayrhan Uul, and its summit is 14,311 feet (4,362 meters) above sea level. The Mongol Altai is the only place where glaciers are found today in Mongolia. A smaller range, the Gobi Altai, branches off from the Mongol Altai to the southwest.

The second range, the Khangai Mountains, runs from northwest to southeast near the center of Mongolia. Although the Khangai has several peaks taller than 12,000 feet (3,500 meters), it also has many gentle slopes covered with good pastureland. A spur of this range, called the Khubsugal Mountains, runs northward into the Soviet Union. Lake Khubsugal, near the border, is the deepest lake in central Asia (1,781 feet; 238 meters). It lies in a region of steep cliff formations, many mountain lakes, and huge subterranean caverns.

The third major mountain range of Mongolia, the Khentei, is less rugged than the other two and rises northeast of Ulan Bator. The Khentei surrounds the capital city and has peaks that reach heights of 8,000 feet.

Between and among these mountain ranges lie deep, scenic valleys and gorges. Although few people live in them, these basins offer some of the country's most dramatic and beautiful landscapes. In addition, many plant and animal species flourish there.

Between the Altai and Khangai ranges on the country's northern frontier lies an area known as the Great Lakes Basin. It contains more than 300 lakes. Another deep valley lies between the Khangai and Khentei ranges. Called the Tuul Gor-Orhon Gor Basin, this fertile area is believed to be the site of the very earliest Mongol settlements. The valley floor is strewn with ancient ruins.

The Khorgo region, on the northern flanks of the Khangai Mountains, contains half a dozen extinct volcanoes and many lakes that lie in the craters of old volcanoes. One of these lakes, Terhiyn Tsagaan Lake, is 24 square miles in area and lies at a high altitude (6,760 feet; 2,060 meters). A small island in this lake is a famous bird sanctuary. Near the source of the Orhon River, also in the Khangai range, is another volcanic area with many hot springs. Here too is found the White Stallion River, which flows so rapidly in its deep gorge that it produces a constant roar.

Mongolia contains more than 3,000 lakes larger than half a square mile. Most of them are located in the mountain-and-basin regions of the north and west. One of the most beautiful lakes is Lake Bayan, on the western flank of the Khangai Mountains. It is edged with golden sand dunes and harbors many varieties of birds and fish. Legend says that an ancient city vanished into the depths of the lake—and archaeological remains dredged from the lake bed by modern scientists have given some truth to the legend.

The country is also rich in rivers. Some streams and rivers are seasonal, flowing only during the spring snow-melts or summer rains. Often these streams vanish into the sand or stone of the southern desert. In the north, however, the mountain streams merge into deep rivers. They flow swiftly and steeply, and they

The exotic snow leopard, which lives in the northern mountains, changes its color with the seasons

have much potential as sources of hydroelectric energy. There are three major rivers: the Selenga, which drains northward into Lake Baikal in the Soviet Union; the Onon, which flows eastward and finally empties into the Pacific Ocean; and the Kobdo, which flows westward from the glaciers of the Altai into central Asia. A smaller river, the Tuul, runs through Ulan Bator.

Plant and animal life is abundant in the mountainous regions of Mongolia. The northern slopes especially are heavily forested. The most common tree is the Siberian larch, but cedar, spruce, birch, aspen, and poplar are also found. The forests harbor lynx, Asiatic red deer, elk, brown bear, the rare and beautiful snow leopard, wolverine, boar (a type of large, fierce wild pig), squirrel, and sable (a small weasel-like animal prized for its fine fur). Ducks,

geese, pelicans, and other water birds throng the lakes; condors and golden eagles nest in the high crags. Salmon, trout, perch, pike, and other varieties of fish are found in the lakes and rivers.

The central and eastern part of Mongolia is covered by steppe plains, or grasslands. Toward the east, the terrain is quite hilly, and many hills reach heights of 2,300 feet. This part of the country also has many small, stubby rock formations, which are the cones of extinct volcanoes. The Dariganga district, located in the far eastern tip of Mongolia, contains more than 220 such volcanic remains. Toward the south, vast level plains carry the steppes into the northern fringes of the Gobi. In all, the characteristic treeless steppe landscape, with its wide, flat horizon and big sky, makes up nearly three-quarters of Mongolia's territory.

Many types of grasses grow on the steppes, and in summer the grasslands are carpeted with brilliant red, yellow, violet, and blue wildflowers. Animals native to the steppes include the fleet-footed Mongolian gazelle and the marmot (a fur-bearing animal about the size of a rabbit). The steppes are also the home of Mongolia's vast grazing herds of domesticated animals. Sheep, cattle, goats, yaks in the north, and camels in the south roam the grasslands in immense numbers. Of course, there are also many large herds of horses. It is an old adage that wherever you find a Mongolian, there you will also find at least two horses.

The Gobi Desert

The feature of Mongolia best known to the rest of the world is probably the Gobi Desert. But most of the traditional images that you may think of when you hear the word "desert" do not apply to the Gobi. The Gobi is never very hot, but can be bitterly cold, especially at night. And there are no palm trees and very little sand. In fact, most of the Gobi region isn't really desert at all.

Mongolians do not speak of "the Gobi." Rather, they refer to "a *gobi*," which is their word for an area of hard, flat soil covered with gravel and sparse vegetation. Most of the region known as the Gobi—especially the part that borders on the central steppes—has enough vegetation to support camels, goats, and horses, although it is drier than the steppes themselves. This topography is sometimes called "semi-desert." Three kinds of small trees grow near water-holes and streambeds here: the white-barked *zag*, which sometimes reaches eight feet in height; the *turai*, which resembles a small oak; and the *tamarack* or tamarisk, a tree which is found throughout Asia. The tamarack's pink blossoms are the same shade as the *saksaul* plant, a hardy weed that covers much of the Gobi. Together, the tamarack and the saksaul give the desert landscape a distinctive pink tinge.

This hand-powered pump brings needed water to the surface of the Gobi

Although there are no rivers in this part of Mongolia, seasonal streams occasionally form water-holes in years of unusually heavy rainfall. Sometimes, too, rare thunderstorms cause flash floods similar to those of the American Southwest. There are also many springs in the semi-desert lands. Throughout this part of the Gobi, fresh water lies close beneath the land's surface and can easily be reached by shallow wells.

Only in the far south, near the border with the People's Republic of China, does the Gobi become a true desert. Here there is almost no vegetation and the land supports little or no life. Sand covers about 15 percent of this area, especially in the east. Dunes in this part of Mongolia are often 1,000 feet (175 meters) high. When the spring winds blow from the east across the miles of dunes, huge sandstorms are born. Sometimes these storms darken the skies over Ulan Bator for days at a time.

Przewalski's wild horse is found in the semi-deserts of Central Asia

The Gobi contains several striking natural features. In the eastern and central parts of the region, strange rock formations exist—huge columns of basalt (a hard volcanic rock) that look like clusters of giant six-sided pencils. Three small mountain ranges in the southern Gobi are called the Gov Gurvan Saikhan, which means "Three Gobi Beauties." This part of Mongolia is rich in fossils. During the 1920s and 1930s, a famous scientist and explorer named Roy Chapman Andrews roamed the Gobi, collecting specimens for the American Museum of Natural History in New York. At a place called the Flaming Cliffs in the Gov Gurvan Saikhan, he found dinosaur eggs 95 million years old.

The Yelyn Am ("Valley of Condors") is also located in the south Gobi. It is an area of rocky cliffs and deep chasms. Many

This camp on the edge of the Gobi will be moved
when the herds have eaten all the grass in the area

condors live there, and the Mongolian government has made the Yelyn Am into a national park so that the nests of the condors will always be protected.

The semi-desert regions of the northern, central, and western Gobi are home to many species of animals, some of them found nowhere else in the world. Among them are the *argal* (Mongolian wild sheep), *kulan* (Mongolian wild ass), wild camel, *mazalai* (Gobi bear), and a rare ancestor of the modern horse called Przewalski's wild horse. There are huge black vultures, whose wingspan may be greater than six feet. Ibex (a kind of antelope) and gazelles are common. Although the Mongolian gazelle is small, it covers great distances, easily achieving running speeds of 40 miles an hour. In addition, many herdsmen travel with their graz-

45

ing herds and flocks over the semi-desert portions of the Gobi. Fewer animal species are found in the south Gobi, although some snakes and small rodents live there.

The Gobi Desert has long been thought of as a desolate, inhospitable wasteland. It is true that there are large tracts of dreary, lifeless desert in the Gobi, including the part that lies in Inner Mongolia, in China. But Mongolians have always lived in the

A cluster of gers in the Gobi is dwarfed by the vastness of the desert

Gobi, traveling with their herds and surviving on a diet of meat and milk, although never making permanent settlements there. It was the Western explorers of the 18th and 19th centuries, lacking the special survival skills of the native nomads, who gave the Gobi its evil reputation. Today, as you will discover later in this book, the Gobi is slowly being transformed into a settled and productive territory.

The People of Mongolia

In the 19th century, early anthropologists (scientists who study the cultures of various peoples) divided the human race into three broad groups: the Negroid, the Caucasian, and the Mongolian or Oriental-Asiatic. Although today we know that this grouping of human types is too general to be accurate, the term "Mongolian" or "Mongoloid" is still sometimes broadly used to refer to all Oriental, Siberian, and Eskimo people.

The true Mongolians—direct descendants of the original Mongol tribes—have some characteristics in common with Native Americans. (It is likely that the Mongols, the Native Americans, and the Eskimos all originated in the same central Asian tribes, early in prehistoric times.) The Mongolians have yellow-gold to dark brown skin, high cheekbones, slanted eyes, and dark brown or black eyes and hair. They are generally more ruggedly built and strong-featured than their neighbors, the Chinese. About one-tenth of the population of Mongolia, however, is indistinguishable from the Chinese; these people have round faces and short noses. Most Mongolians are short and wiry, although quite a few of them are six feet tall or more.

Although true Mongols, or Khalka Mongols, as they are

48

called, make up more than three-quarters of the population today, there are also sizable numbers of other groups living in Mongolia. Most of them are closely related to the Mongols in culture and history. They include Russians, Torgut (Siberian Eskimos), and such central Asian peoples as the Buryat, Dariganga, Uryankhai, and Dzakchin tribespeople.

The largest non-Mongol group in Mongolia consists of about 60,000 people called Kazakhs, who live in the far western region of the country. They are members of a tribe that lives primarily in the Republic of Kazakhstan, in Soviet Central Asia, and has traded with the Mongols by caravan for centuries. The smallest non-Mongol group is the Tsaatan. They are related to the Eskimo people of Siberia. A few of them dwell in the high mountain forests of northern Mongolia, where they live principally by herding reindeer.

With the exception of the Kazakhs, who speak a language of their own, all these groups speak Mongolian. If you were to travel through Mongolia from east to west, you would hear many varying dialects, or versions, of the basic language. Although they might sound like different languages to you, a Mongolian would be able to understand them all. Mongolians also love learning other languages and usually find it easy to do so. Maybe they are fond of different languages because they have been at the crossroads of northern Asia for so long. As warriors, and later as traders, they had to learn to communicate with many other peoples. Today, the university in Ulan Bator teaches Russian, Chinese, Tibetan, Manchu, and English.

The horse-post riders carried messages in embroidered saddlebags like these

The ancient Mongol script was written vertically and from left to right. In the 1940s, it was replaced by the Cyrillic alphabet, which is used to write Russian. Two special characters had to be invented to represent sounds that occur in Mongolian but not in Russian.

Mongolians seem to share a "national personality." As a group, they are a hardworking, cheerful people. Drawing on a long nomad tradition of hospitality to strangers and travelers, they are friendly and polite. Guests are always made welcome and treated to the best refreshments the household has to offer.

Mongolians are also somewhat formal in their dress. They tend to disapprove of the informal clothing and sportswear often worn by foreign technicians or travelers in their country. The traditional Mongolian garment for both sexes is the *del,* a long, coat-like garment with a stand-up collar. It can be made of either cotton, wool, or silk, and is often padded with fur during cold weather. Dels worn on special occasions, such as weddings or holidays, are often beautifully embroidered with traditional designs in many colors. The del is worn over loose cotton trousers or sheepskin leggings.

Traditional Mongolian garb includes a sheepskin del, a spiked cap, and a richly embroidered waistcoat

Western-style clothing—suits for men and dresses in dark colors for women—is also acceptable in Mongolia today, especially among city dwellers. Pedestrians on the streets of Ulan Bator and other cities wear both old-fashioned and modern outfits.

In the six decades since the founding of the Mongolian People's Republic, many changes have taken place in the population of Mongolia. For one thing, it has increased to two million. The population is continuing to grow at a rate of 3 percent each year. This is one of the highest growth rates in Asia. In fact, while many Asian countries are trying to lower their growth rates because of overpopulation and poor standards of living, the Mongolians are trying to increase their numbers rapidly. They believe that their country can support many more people, and that a larger population is necessary to help modernize Mongolia. For this reason, parents are encouraged to have large families and are rewarded with government assistance and cash bonuses for each child. A mother of ten children earns as much just for being a parent as a skilled factory worker earns on the job.

The way people make their living has also changed dramatically since the Mongolian Revolution. In 1925, almost 87 percent of the people in the country were livestock breeders or their families. Landowners and priests made up 13 percent of the total. Today, less than 1 percent of the people are priests, all land is owned by the state, and only about half of the population consists of livestock breeders and their families. The rest of the Mongolians belong to a category that did not exist in 1925 but now makes up half the population: urban workers and their families. This change

Half the people of Mongolia are animal herders; despite some modernization, they follow the traditional way of life

is one of the most important aspects of life in Mongolia today. Although no one would deny the importance of the herdsmen, the educated, city-dwelling Mongolians, many of whom work in factories or government offices, have a greater say in the direction of national policies.

Another important feature of modern Mongolian life has to do with age. Because the population has grown so rapidly in recent decades, one Mongolian in two is under 25 years old. Demographers (people who study statistics about a country's population and predict trends) say that the average age of the Mongolian population will continue to drop during the coming decades. It is expected that young people will become more and more important in the country's political and cultural life. Some people

fear that the result will be a gradual loss of the traditional way of life—that offices and motorcycles will entirely replace gers and horses. Many young Mongolians today, however, have successfully combined traditional and modern aspects of life. A man or woman who works in a high-rise office building during the day may come home to a ger in the evening. In Ulan Bator and other cities, "suburbs" of gers contain many families who prefer them to more modern houses or apartments.

This family's ger is furnished with a traditional hand-made chest

Hatgal, a town in the far north, is a good example of how Mongolians manage to blend the old and the new. Many nomads gave up their wandering ways to come to work in Hatgal's big sawmill. They clung to their nomadic homes, however, and set up their gers in a large encampment on the edge of town. Because tent dwellers are used to the privacy of the wide-open steppes, where large distances often separate the nearest neighbors, they have constructed fences between each ger at Hatgal. The encampment is wired, so the residents have electricity. Because they pay no rent, the gers are cheaper than apartments, and many of the workers are able to afford television, still a comparatively new luxury in Mongolia. It is not uncommon to enter a ger that is furnished with old, handmade wooden chests and stools, large sheepskin pillows, a wood-burning stove for cooking—and a radio or TV set.

Government and Education

The Mongolian People's Revolutionary Party is the only political party in Mongolia. It governs through *khurals,* or committees, of deputies at all levels. The national khural, which is called the Great People's Khural, is like a parliament. It is the highest governing body in the land and consists of one representative for every 4,000 people. A nine-member presidium, or committee, is the governing body when the Great Khural is not in session. The members of the Great Khural elect the Supreme Court, which administers Mongolia's laws.

Smaller khurals govern the 18 *aymaks,* or provinces, of Mongolia. Each aymak also has its own court. Towns have khurals and courts, too. Each khural consists of deputies elected from the local population, and the khurals elect the judges. The aymaks are divided into smaller units, called *somons,* and still smaller ones, called *hurins.* The hurin is about the size of the average county in the United States.

Land and livestock in the hurins have been collectivized on the Soviet model, which means that they belong jointly to all of the citizens in the hurin, who form what is called a cooperative farm or ranch. The local khural decides when a herdsman should move, sell, or butcher his animals, and each herder's profits are shared by all. But the state does permit each herder to keep a certain number of animals for his own personal use and profit. In the north, that number is 50; in the south, 70. The herder may sell or breed these animals in whatever way he chooses.

The Mongolian People's Revolutionary Party (MPRP) is the oldest governing communist party outside the Soviet Union. It has almost 60,000 members. A young people's branch of the MPRP, called Revsomol, has about 90,000 members. The party also sponsors a Young Pioneer organization for children. The Young Pioneers attend club meetings and summer camps organized on communist principles.

The Organization of Mongolian Women is a symbol of the new Mongolia. Although women had few rights in pre-revolutionary Mongolia, the Mongolian People's Republic was one of the first Asian countries to grant them full economic and political equality. Women hold many jobs today, from airline pilots to scientific researchers to doctors. One-fourth of the members of the Great Khural are women.

Another important organization is the association of trade unions, which has nearly a quarter of a million members. The unionists help the Great Khural decide how to develop the country's resources and promote industry and trade with other nations.

Of the many changes that the modern Mongolian government has made in the life of the people, one of the most significant is health care. In 1925, there were only two doctors, five medical assistants, and three nurses in the entire country. Fifty years later,

The town hall of a collective is the center of political and social activity

*Dogs help herders
keep track of their
livestock*

there was one hospital bed for every 100 people and one doctor
for every 550 people—more than in many well-developed Euro-
pean countries.

All medical and dental care is free. Each aymak has at least
one hospital, and every somon has a hospital or first-aid station.
Doctors and nurses frequently visit their more isolated patients by
means of helicopters or small planes, which can land almost any-
where on the firm surface of the steppes.

Although Mongolian hospitals feature new equipment and
Western-trained doctors, traditional folk remedies and Oriental

medicines are also used to good effect. Acupuncture—the ancient Chinese practice of relieving pain by lightly inserting small needles into the skin at certain points—is commonplace in Mongolia. Hot mineral baths are often prescribed for such ailments as rheumatism and influenza.

Some of the hot volcanic springs of Mongolia have been used for medical purposes for centuries. A famous one is located in the Hatan Hayrhan, a heart-shaped mountain in the western Gobi. Over the years, the spring has carved seven deep basins in the rock. They are called the Kettles of Hatan Hayrhan, and people come from miles away to bathe in them. Another famous medicinal spring is found just south of the ancient site of Karakorum. It is called Hujirtu, which means "Soda Place," because the water is almost like hot bicarbonate of soda. Today, 3,000 people each year wash away their aches and pains at Hujirtu. Perhaps Ogadai and the other khans did so, too, after a hard day in the saddle.

A Revolution in Education

Just as it brought health care to the masses, the revolution transformed education in Mongolia. In 1921, the country contained one small general school and not a single secondary school or college. Buddhist lamas received clerical training, usually in Tibetan, which was not available to the ordinary tribesman.

By the early 1970s, almost all Mongolians could read and write. Six hundred general and secondary schools and 20 vocational and technical schools had been built. Five universities also existed: the Mongolian State University in Ulan Bator (established

A professor discusses natural history with students at the University of Ulan Bator

in 1942, with departments of physics, mathematics, chemistry, biology, social sciences, economics, and language), the Higher Party School (where students specialize in communist doctrine), and colleges of teaching, medicine, and agricultural studies. There are also two Russian language schools in Ulan Bator.

Education is free in Mongolia. It is also compulsory, which means that by law children must attend school, just as in the United States. Children who live in cities attend for ten years, beginning at age eight. Children who live in gers on the steppes attend for eight years, also beginning at age eight. Because many gers are isolated from communities with schools, seven out of ten ger children attend boarding schools. The school year runs from September through May. Schoolchildren wear western-style uniforms: brown corduroy coats and pants for the boys and brown dresses, covered with white or black aprons, for the girls. Boys and girls frequently wear red bandannas tied around their necks.

Children who do well in school and want to continue their education in technical school or college must pass strict entrance exams. If they score highly, the state pays all costs for their higher education. Increasing numbers of Mongolian students are attending colleges and universities abroad, especially in the Soviet Union and other communist countries. Today there are 104 college students for every 10,000 inhabitants in Mongolia—exactly double France's ratio.

Mongolians stroll a square in Ulan Bator, the nation's capital

Ulan Bator and Other Cities

Because Mongolia's people have been nomadic tent dwellers for much of their history, the country contains few cities and towns and almost no truly old structures. Urban Mongolia is only a few decades old.

The one ancient city that was inhabited in historical times, Karakorum, was destroyed and never rebuilt, although some Buddhist shrines were erected near the site in the 1600s. Today the administrative buildings of a vast cooperative farm stand where Ogadai Khan's proud imperial capital once stood.

Ulan Bator is not only the capital of the Mongolian People's Republic, but also the most important industrial and urban center in the country. The old city, Urga, was founded on the present site in 1639 as the home of the Living Buddha. At the time of the revolution in 1921, it had a population of 60,000, including many lamas. The city was nothing more than a cluster of adobe monasteries surrounded by gers. In fact, it was called "the city of felt" because of the felt walls of the gers. Within a few decades, however, the city of felt had become a city of steel and glass. Now it is home to half a million people—one in every four Mongolians lives in Ulan Bator.

Because it was a planned city and did not grow up haphazardly over a long period of time, Ulan Bator is spacious and efficient. It features broad avenues, well-organized apartment complexes (so many high-rise apartment buildings have been built with Soviet loans in recent years that the Mongolians refer to them as "Brezhnev's gifts"), and administrative centers. Ulan Bator is now in the final stages of a 20-year development program designed to divide the city into 19 districts, each with its own theaters, stores, and governing bodies.

Sukhe Bator Square, in the center of Ulan Bator, is named for the revolutionary hero. The capitol building where the Great Khural meets is located on the square. It is an impressive structure with white marble columns. The city also has a large, new sports stadium and a modern, glass-walled exhibition hall and arena where agricultural and artistic events are held. The exhibition hall is of special interest because its pagoda-style roof was modeled on that of the Temple of Generous Mercy, one of the old buildings still standing in Ulan Bator. The temple was a Buddhist shrine, built in 1905 at a cost of three and a half tons of silver and decorated with carved demons. It now serves as a religious museum.

Mongolia's first department store, called simply "Big Store," was built in Ulan Bator in the early 1960s. Six stories high and as large as a city block, it proved popular with shoppers even though it had no escalators or elevators and patrons had to climb stairs with their purchases. Newer stores have now been built in Ulan Bator and several other cities.

Even more noteworthy than its stores are Ulan Bator's factor-

A crowd of consumers gathers at an outdoor bookstall in the central square of Ulan Bator; in front of the parliament building in the background stands a statue of Sukhe Bator on horseback

67

ies. Sixty years ago, there was no such thing as a factory in Mongolia. Today there are many, most of them in Ulan Bator. They are usually built by other communist countries, who send technicians to train the Mongolian workers and receive the finished products in payment. An example is the Wilhelm Pieck Carpet Factory, named for an East German political hero. Built by the East Germans for the Mongolians, it uses up-to-date machinery to weave rugs in old-fashioned tribal designs.

The best view of Ulan Bator is from a nearby peak of the Khentei Mountains, which surround the city. From the peak, you can look down over the streets and buildings that flow along both banks of the Tuul River toward the outlying fringes of gers and the open land beyond them. At the top of the peak is Ulan Bator's grandest monument, a huge mosaic-and-stone tribute to the Soviet soldiers who died in the Mongolian Revolution.

Mongolia's second city is Darhan, which lies between Ulan Bator and the Soviet border. It is even newer than Ulan Bator; its foundation stone was laid in 1961. At that time, 1,500 people lived in tents at the site. By 1980, more than 56,000 workers, many of them young people, had flocked to Darhan to find jobs in its coal and iron mines and steel industry. As a center of manufacturing, Darhan almost rivals Ulan Bator. Schools, hospitals, and apartment buildings have been built for the workers and their families, and Darhan continues to grow rapidly.

The third largest industrial center is the city of Suhbaatar, established in 1937 and named for Sukhe Bator. Located almost on the border with the Soviet Union, Suhbaatar is an important railway center as well as a manufacturing location. Choibalsan, in the east, is another new industrial complex, also named to commemorate a revolutionary hero. Dzuun-bayan, in the eastern Gobi, sprang up recently in an area of concentrated oil drilling and mining. Uliastay and Hovd are the principal cities of western Mongolia. Smaller urban centers are scattered throughout the country, with at least one in each aymak.

Looking toward the future, Mongolia's government planners expect cities and towns to keep growing. They believe that more and more Mongolians will live in urban centers and will work in industrial or professional jobs. In short, they want Mongolia to follow the pattern of western industrial countries. At this point, the Mongolian people do appear to favor urbanization. But they also have a long tradition of independence and closeness to the land. It remains to be seen whether the nomadic tradition will continue to remain strong in a large segment of the population.

Resources, Economy, and Communication

Mongolia contains many natural resources suitable for an industrial state. Because the country's economy has always been one of simple herding, most of these resources were not exploited—or even discovered—until recently. Now it appears that Mongolia has the potential to become one of the richest countries in Asia.

Geological surveys have shown that Mongolia contains large deposits of iron, tin, copper, gold, and silver, as well as a number of lesser-known minerals (such as wolframite) that are important in some industrial processes. These minerals are now being mined and either used in Mongolia's own manufacturing programs or exported. The country is one of the world's biggest exporters of fluorspar, a mineral used in the making of steel and industrial acid. Most of the fluorspar, along with quantities of copper and molybdenum (another rare metal), are exported to the Soviet Union.

Large deposits of coal have also been found, although development of these resources is just beginning. Coal is mined at Darhan and at Nalaykha, east of Ulan Bator. In the 1950s, a large oil refinery was built at Sayn Shand, in the south Gobi near the Chinese border. Oil production has fallen off recently, and the Mongolians hope to develop other sources of power for the coming years. Hydroelectric energy for factories will come from damming the swift mountain rivers of the north, and gers and buildings may use solar heaters to take advantage of Mongolia's blue skies.

Another resource is the teeming wildlife, which contributes to the economy in several ways. Fur-bearing animals, especially the marmots of the steppes, are hunted for their pelts. The fur industry brings much foreign money into Mongolia. Government programs have been set up to encourage fishing in the northern lakes. Several commercial fisheries now export whitefish, salmon,

The day's catch is rowed to shore by the crew of a fishing boat

Fishermen in Baikal-Kudarin dry their nets at day's end

and other products. The fishermen work even in the bitter cold of winter; often they simply unload their catch on the shore and let nature freeze it for them. Although Mongolians do not as a rule eat fish, some of the younger people are beginning to include fish in their diet.

Hunting is another source of income. Mongolia's wild rivers and empty plains are very appealing to sportsmen, who must pay the government a fee for a hunting license. The Mongolian Hunts-

men's Association has 30,000 members, who annually kill between two and three million animals. Even more lucrative is the growing business of catering to foreign hunters, wealthy Europeans or Americans who pay as much as 16,000 U.S. dollars for a one-week chance to shoot an ibex or wild deer.

Despite its eagerness to exploit its wildlife resources, however, Mongolia has taken precautions to safeguard them as well. Conservation laws impose limits on all hunting and fishing activities, and large tracts in many parts of the country have been set aside as national parks and wildlife reservations.

Mongolia's greatest resource—although no longer the sole support of its economy—is its domestic animal herds. According to old pre-revolutionary records, the country held about nine million domestic animals in 1918: sheep, goats, horses, cattle, and camels. By 1980, that figure had increased to 24 million. Animal products are the country's biggest exports. Mongolia sends meat, butter, live animals, hides, and wool to other communist countries, mostly to the Soviet Union. Mongolia also engages in some

Sheep dips, like this electrically powered one in Northern Mongolia, keep herds free of disease

trade with China, bartering horses for cloth, electronics, and other consumer goods.

Because of the economic importance of the herds, government-sponsored programs have urged progress in veterinary science and animal breeding technology. For example, scientists have perfected the breeding of the *hainag,* a first-generation cross between a yak and a cow, which is beginning to take the place of cattle on the steppes. It produces more milk than either of its parents. And, on an experimental farm south of Ulan Bator, tall American horses are being crossbred with the smaller native Mongolian horses in an attempt to create a breed that is large but still hardy enough for Mongolia's climate.

Agriculture has been transformed in Mongolia in the decades since 1921. At that time, there were really no farms in the country. The nomads occasionally tended gardens for a year or two, and there were orchards at some of the southern oases, but land was never farmed permanently. The country's new leaders recognized that modern, scientific farming can feed more people per acre than can be fed if the land is used solely for grazing purposes, so huge collective farms were established. Now there are approximately 300 such farms in Mongolia.

Huge tracts of virgin land were plowed and new crops were sown, often with Soviet-made farm machinery. By the early 1970s, Mongolia produced enough wheat to meet the needs of its people. In 1981, nearly one and a half million acres were planted in wheat. Vegetables are also being grown, and more Mongolians are becoming accustomed to eating them. As the amount of land

Veterinary science is essential to Mongolia's herding industry; here, a veterinarian vaccinates cattle

available for grazing is reduced by farming and industry, the production of food for the herds—hay and oats—has also become an important part of agriculture.

Mongolian agriculturists are making a determined attempt to tame the Gobi—or at least a small part of it. Many hundreds of wells have been drilled in the semi-desert regions of the Gobi, and the natural underground reservoirs are being tapped to fill irrigation canals on farms. Fruit, vegetables, and food for livestock now grow in neat rows where once only nomads, camels, and wild deer roamed.

Now that many rural Mongolians have become farmers instead of wandering herdsmen, new animals have been introduced. In the old nomadic days, pigs and chickens were extremely rare in Mongolia, although they were common in neighboring China. Most Mongolians of two generations ago had never seen a pig. In fact, one of their children's stories tells of a clever wolf who huffs and puffs trying to blow down the ger of the four little goats—this is the same story that American readers call "The Three Little Pigs." Today, piggeries and chicken farms are numerous on the steppes and in the northern valleys.

The past six decades have seen much investment in industrial and manufacturing facilities, as well as many new methods and products in agriculture. All in all, agriculture (including both farming and herding) still makes up more than half of the total economy of Mongolia. But government planners say that very soon the country's annual production will be evenly divided between industry and agriculture.

Although Mongolia now imports (buys from other nations) more products than it exports (sells to other nations), the country's current economic plan calls for a balance of exports and imports in another decade or so.

The Mongolian unit of currency is the *togrog*, which is divided into 100 *mongo*. The togrog is closely linked in value to the Soviet Union's ruble.

All connections between Mongolia and the rest of the world go through the Soviet Union, which administers Mongolia's international telephone, telegraph, and mail systems. The Soviet Union also developed the key links in the modern transportation system that has helped Mongolian business and industry develop.

In 1921, the only ways to travel or transport goods were by horseback, carts, or camel caravans. The first transportation company was set up in 1925. Unfortunately, it had almost no money and only seven old vehicles. In 1929, however, the Soviets joined with the Mongolians to form Mongoltrans, a company that built roads and bridges and operated a freight service. The company was turned over to the Mongolians in 1936 and renamed Mongoltransport. By that time, it employed 1,000 people and owned 300 vehicles.

Steamboats began to carry freight up and down the larger rivers in the mid-1920s. Because of the short, steep nature of many of Mongolia's waterways, however, their importance in transportation has remained limited. Trains proved to be much more important. By 1956, the Trans-Mongolian Railway had been completed. It runs between the northern and southern borders, passing through Darhan and Ulan Bator, and links the Soviet Union's Trans-Siberian Railway with the Chinese rail system. The railway has been a key factor in Mongolia's economic development; more than three-fourths of the country's freight traffic is carried by train. A network of other railways connects most of the aymaks.

Air services were introduced in the early 1940s. At first they were limited to emergency medical evacuations and government business, but by 1970 commercial flights connected all the aymaks and many of the somons and state farms. Today nearly a quarter of all people who travel within Mongolia do so by air.

For centuries, Mongolia was a land where travel was slow, governed by the pace of the browsing herds. Now roads, railways, and a domestic airline have made it a smaller place, and its people are becoming accustomed to the pace of 20th-century life.

Culture and Customs

Like everything else in Mongolia, the cultural life is a unique blend of the old and the new. A good example is Mongolia's literature.

The works of modern novelists, such as Damdinsuren, are popular at home and are beginning to attract attention in the outside world. During the 1930s, the poems and stories of Natsagorj were widely read. *The Old Scribe's Story,* the autobiography of writer Navaannamzhil, was an important publication of the 1940s.

In addition to these contemporary works, most Mongolians still love to repeat their centuries-old folktales. Many of these tales, which are a little bit like the *Arabian Nights,* feature Badarcha, a roguish, wandering lama. Stories of Badarcha's humorous exploits are told in the gers on chilly evenings when the family huddles around the stove for warmth. In the Gobi region, other folktales tell of Almas, a legendary half-man, half-beast, something like the famous Abominable Snowman of Tibet.

Other traditional types of literature are still popular: the *yurol* (poetry of good wishes), the *magtaal* (poetry of praise), and the *tsam* and *maidari* (religious plays inspired by Tibetan Buddhism). Mongolian chess is very old and still popular. Beautifully carved chess sets have khans for kings, dogs for queens, and camels for

A bull and yak lock borns in a wood carving by artist Gebschi

bishops. The ancient arts of pottery and weaving are still prac-
ticed. In particular, Mongolian artists continue to make *shirdegs,*
richly ornamented felt rugs that were used to decorate the
entrances to gers as early as the 13th century.

The Mongolians are also passionately fond of music. In fact,
they have a saying that Mongolia invented music for the rest of the
world. Although many people attend concerts of the State Symphony Orchestra in Ulan Bator, older, more traditional forms of
music are still played throughout the country. One is a type of
singing called the "long song," not because the song itself goes on
for a long time, but because the singer lingers on every syllable,
drawing out the words for a sad, plaintive effect. These songs are
usually about life on the steppes and the loneliness of Mongolia's
vast distances. The so-called "short songs" (which may actually be

longer than the long songs) are cheerful and usually humorous; people often dance to them.

One other type of song is found only in Mongolia. It is called the *hoomi,* and it is sung by men who have been specially trained to control the muscles of their throats and abdomens. When they sing, they seem to be producing several notes at once. The effect is eerie and beautiful.

These folksongs are accompanied on an instrument native to Mongolia, the *morin khour,* which is a little bit like a two-stringed violin. It is hand-carved, decorated with a wooden horse's head, and played with a horsehair bow. Legend says that an ancient nobleman loved his favorite horse so much that when the horse died, he invented the morin khour and strung it with hairs from

Most Mongolians can play the traditional instrument, the morin khour

the horse's mane and tail, using it to accompany him as he sang of his grief. Morin khour music today ranges from formal chamber concerts to spontaneous neighborhood sing-alongs.

Troupes of dancers also preserve many ancient folk dances of the Mongol people, including a complicated courtship dance in which both the man and the woman must balance wine cups on their heads and hands. These dances are usually performed in magnificently decorated Manchu-style costumes.

Rare and valuable Mongolian manuscripts are housed in the Central State Library in Ulan Bator

Although all Mongolians know the stories and legends of Genghis Khan and the Mongol World Empire, in all of Mongolia there is no memorial to him. The State Museum in Ulan Bator, however, houses several very ancient standards (personal symbols carried into battle by warlords) that are said to have been Genghis's own. One is a huge three-pointed brass spear, trimmed in silver. Two others are single-pointed spears, one trimmed with white horsehair, the other with black. They are so large that most men cannot lift them, let alone carry them on horseback. Other cultural relics, including statues made by Zanabazar, a famous 17th-century artist, are on view in the Bogdo Genen Palace Museum. It is a large collection of folk art housed in the former winter palace of the khan, built in 1898.

Ulan Bator boasts Mongolia's own movie studio, where the government produces films (mostly political or educational ones, although some are epic adventure stories) that are shown at state theaters in every city and on the larger farms. The State Central Library in Ulan Bator contains a priceless collection of more than a million volumes, many of them very ancient Tibetan and Mongol manuscripts. Ulan Bator also has a circus, a puppet theater, the State Drama Theater, and the State Opera and Ballet Theater. Many amateur dramatic and musical groups are active in the smaller cities and towns.

One other institution in Ulan Bator preserves part of the country's past. It is the Gandan Monastery—the only functioning Buddhist monastery left in Mongolia (many other monasteries remain standing but have been put to other uses). Gandan consists of a cluster of pagoda-roofed buildings surrounded by a high wall. The lamas, who shave their heads and dress in yellow robes, seldom leave Gandan, but all citizens are welcome to visit the monastery to attend the services or to meditate or pray. One in every hundred boys who wishes to become a priest is accepted. Although the government officially discourages religion, it does not ban participation in religious activities, and Gandan is allowed to remain open in honor of the importance of Buddhism in Mongolia's history.

Old Mongolia is kept alive in the most famous traditional celebration, the Naadam, which has existed in some form for at least 2,300 years. The Naadam, or Festival of the Three Manly Sports, takes place for three days each year, beginning on July 11, Mongolia's independence day.

The first day's sport is wrestling, performed in the old-fashioned Mongol style. The many hundreds of participants wear brightly colored, snug leather vests. In pairs, they struggle to make each other lose their footing. A single match may take half a day, but Mongolians never tire of watching the wrestlers. (Modern free-style wrestling, introduced in 1962, also has many fans.) The winners are awarded such titles as Lion, Elephant, and Falcon; a three-time winner is an Invincible Titan.

On the second day, archers compete individually and in teams for such titles as Most Scrupulous Archer and Miraculous Bowman. They use wood-and-horn bows of ancient design and shoot at old, leather-covered targets.

The third day is the most spectacular and exciting. It is a 20-mile

Lavishly embroidered Manchu-style costumes, like these worn by turn-of-the-century aristocrats, are still worn during the ritual courtship dance

cross-country horse race for children from seven to twelve years old. Both boys and girls compete. Horse races for all ages are also held in January and February, the months when Mongolians celebrate the New Year. Such races have a long tradition—Marco Polo wrote that he had once seen 10,000 white horses race at the command of the Great Khan.

Although the government supports the foundation of new and modern cultural organizations, such as the opera and ballet, it also encourages its people to keep their folkways alive. As long as the Naadam and the morin khour are part of life in Mongolia, the old and noble Mongolian heritage will be preserved.

Only one applicant in a hundred is admitted to Gandan Monastery

Ways of Life Today

Sixty-five years ago, almost every Mongolian was either a priest or a member of a herder family. Today Mongolians operate computers in government and business offices, attend medical school, work in industry, and harvest crops. For many of them, though, tending the herds is still the preferred way of life.

For herding families, life is sometimes hard and work is long.

The women milk the mares, camels, or goats. From the mare's milk they make the staple drink airak, usually using a leather churn that must be stirred and shaken often. They also make cheese, yogurt, and a vodka-like drink enjoyed on special occasions. In addition, they clean the gers every day.

Herdsmen usually spend ten hours or more each day in the saddle (or, increasingly, in a truck or on a motorcycle), checking their wide-ranging flocks to be sure that no animals are lost. The herdsman's life is, in fact, surprisingly similar to that of the cowboy in the American Old West, right down to events that resemble rodeos. In cattle-roping contests, though, the herdsmen do not use lassos. Instead, they use the *urga,* a noose on the end of a pole that may be as long as 15 feet.

The gers they live in are usually simple places. The felt walls

Tourists—especially from other communist countries—have begun to visit Mongolia; here, hikers explore the Gobi Altai mountain range

may be lined with lighter cotton. There is little furniture—wooden chests for storing woolens and kitchen utensils are lined along one wall, saddles and tools are kept against the opposite wall. The ribs of a ger are usually made of wood, often painted bright red (although some gers are made in factories today, most often of aluminum). The wooden stools and chests of the ger are usually painted orange—a color which traditionally means good luck to Mongolians.

While the cash income of a herding family may be low, their expenses are also modest. They pay no rent, and many of them inherit their gers from parents or other relatives. Meat, milk, camel hair and sheep's wool for weaving, and leather hides are all free. City-dwellers sometimes envy the herders their uncomplicated existence.

Urban workers, though, do enjoy many advantages not available to their country cousins: apartments, appliances, western-style clothes, theaters, and museums. But the most attractive feature of city life to most Mongolians who choose it is the opportunity to escape the traditional role of the herdsman or his wife and to earn a living in a new way. Women especially have many more career choices in the city than on the steppes. In 1980, almost 80 percent of Ulan Bator's factory workers were women, all of them earning a wage equal to that of the male workers.

Because so many city mothers work, the government provides many day-care centers. Quite often the mother will deliver her children to the day-care center on Monday morning and pick them up at noon on Saturday, when the 46-hour workweek ends.

This painting, entitled After Work, *shows a herdsman and his family enjoying an evening meal in front of their tent*

The daily lives of all the Mongolian people reflect the many changes that have taken place in the country since it entered the modern world in 1921. Some feel that these changes have been for the better; others regret the passing of the old order. Only one thing is certain: Mongolia will continue to change and grow in many ways. But no matter what happens, the steppes and herds and horsemen that have endured for thousands of years will most likely continue to endure.

Index

acupuncture 61
agriculture 75-77
airak 20, 87
Almas 79
Altai Mountains 36
Altan Khan 28
American Museum of Natural
   History 44
Andrews, Roy Chapman 44
animal breeding 57–58, 74–75
animals (indigenous) 39–40, 45–46
argal 45
art 83
asociation of tade uions 58
aymak 57

Badarcha 79
Baikal, Lake 39
basalt 44
Bayan, Lake 38
"Big Store" 66
birds 39–40, 45
blood-feuds 22
Bogdo Genen Palace Museum 83
Buddhism 26, 28, 32, 83–84
Buryat (people) 49

camels 18, 41, 45
Chagatai (Jagatai) Khan 25
chess 79–80
China 25–30 (see also People's
   Republic of China)
Choibalsan (city) 69
Choibalsan (hero) 31–33
climate 35–36
clothing 50–52
communications 77–78
communism 15, 17, 32–33, 58
cooperative farms 57–58
currency 77
Cyrillic alphabet 50

Dalai Lama 28
Damdinsuren 79
dance 82
Darhan 68, 70
Dariganga (district) 40
Dariganga (people) 49
day-care centers 89
del 51
Dzakchin (people) 49
Dzuun-bayan 69

education 16, 31, 61–63

felt 21, 65
Festival of the Three Manly Sports
   (see Naadam)
fish 40, 71–72
Flaming Cliffs 44
fur trade 71

Gandan Monastery 83–84
Genghis Khan 9–10, 22–25, 83
ger 16, 17, 21, 55–56, 87–89
glaciers 36
Gobi Altai 36
Gobi Desert 9, 41–47, 76
Gobi Plateau 36
Golden Horde 25
Gov Gurvan Saikhan 44
Great Lakes Basin 37
Great People's Khural 57, 58, 66
Guyuk Khan 25

hainag 75
Hatan Hayhran 61
Hatgal 56
health care 16, 60–61
herdsmen 29, 52–53, 57–58, 87–89
Higher Party School 63
hoomi 81
horse-post system 24
Hovd 69
Hsiung-nu (Huns) 18
Hujirtu 61
hunting 72–73
hurin 57

ibex 45
industry 16, 66–69, 70

Inner Mongolia 12, 33, 46

Jagatai (Chagatai) Khan 25
Java 26
Jochi Khan 25

Kalmuck Republic 29
kamikaze 26
Karakorum 25, 61, 65
Kazakhs 49
Kazakhstan, Republic of 49
Kettles of Hatan Hayrhan 61
Khalka Mongols 48–49
khan 21
khanate 25
Khangai Mountains 36
Khentei Mountains 37, 68
Khorgo region 37
Khubsugal, Lake 37
Khubsugal Mountains 36
khural 57
Kobdo River 39
Kublai Khan 13, 25–27
kulan 45
kuraltai 22

lama 28–29, 30, 32, 83–84
lamellar 22
Lenin 33
literature 79
Living Buddha of Urga 28,
   30, 33, 65

magtaal 79
maidari 79
Manchu Dynasty 28, 29

94

marmot 40, 71
mazalai 45
minerals 70
Mongke Khan 25
mongo 77
Mongol Altai 36
Mongol World Empire 9, 26, 28
Mongol horse 17, 20–21, 75
Mongolian Huntsmen Association 72–73
Mongolian language 9, 49
Mongolian People's Revolutionary Party (MPRP) 16, 17, 57, 58
Mongolian Revolution 16, 31–32
Mongolian State University 49, 61–63
Mongoltransport 78
Monh Hayrhan Uul 36
monks (see lama)
mourin khour 81–82
music 80–82

Naadam (Festival of the Three Manly Sports) 84–86
Nalaykha 70
Natsagorj 79
Navaannamzhil 79

October Revolution 31
Ogadai Khan 25, 61
Old Scribe's Story, The 79
Onon River 39
Organization of Mongolian Women 58
Orhon River 37
Outer Mongolia 12, 29

People's Republic of China 14, 42, 75
physical appearance of people 48
Polo, Marco 13, 26, 86
population 13, 52
Przewalski's wild horse 45

rainfall 35
Revsomol 58
Russian language 63

saksaul plant 41
Sayn Shand 70
Secret History of the Mongols, The 24, 35
Selenga River 39
shamanism 21
shirdeg 80
snow leopard 39
social structure 21
somon 57
Soviet Union 14, 15, 33, 66, 77, 78
State Central Library 83
State Drama Theater 83
State Museum 83
State Opera and Ballet Theater 83
State Symphony Orchestra 80
Suhbaatar 68–69
Sukhe Bator 31–33, 68
Sukhe Bator Square 66

tamarack (tamarisk) 41
Temple of Generous Mercy 66
Temujin (see Genghis Khan)
Tengri 21
Terhiyn Tsagaan Lake 37

togrog 77
Tolui Khan 25
topography 36–40
Torgut (people) 49
trade 74–75, 77
Trans-Mongolian Railway 78
transportation 77–78
Trans-Siberian Railway 78
trees 39, 41
Tsaatan (people) 49
tsam 79
tsar 29, 31
turai tree 41
Tuul Gor-Orhon Gor Basin 37
Tuul River 39, 68

Ulan Bator 17, 33, 37, 43,
    55, 65–68
Uliastay 69
United Nations 33
United States 33
Urga (city) 28, 33, 65
urga 87

Uryankhai (people) 49

Valley of the Condors (see Yelyn
    Am)
vegetation 40
veterinary science 75
volcanic springs 61
volcanoes 40
Volga River 29
vultures 45

White Stallion River 37
Wijaya, Prince of Java 26
Wilhelm Pieck Carpet Factory 68

yak 18, 40
Yelyn Am 44–45
Young Pioneer organization 58
yurol 79
yurt 16

zag tree 41
Zanabazar 83